CHILLIN' MY WAY TO SUCCESS!

THE PHENOMENAL LIFE OF AN 8-YEAR-OLD ENTREPRENEUR

CHILLIN' MY WAY TO SUCCESS!

THE PHENOMENAL LIFE OF AN 8-YEAR-OLD ENTREPRENEUR

Kinyah Bean

NOAH'S ARK

PUBLISHING

Editors: Rob Birenbaum and Laval Belle

ISBN: 978-0-692938-79-9

This book is dedicated to young people around the world,
B Chill Leaders Tribe,
Eakin Elementary students and teachers,
Flowood Elementary students and teachers,
Vleary Washington, my entire family and
my best friends, Quincee and Laila.

Thank you all so much for always loving and supporting me!

ACKNOWLEDGMENTS

I would like to express my gratitude to Damon Jones, Keecia Henderson, Rob Birenbaum and Toni Davis for their sponsorship, love and support. I would also like to give my deepest thanks and appreciation to Laval Belle, Stephanie Shelling, Sharon Hogg and my family for their consistent encouragement and support on this journey.

You all ROCK!

LETTER FROM DADDY

Dear My Princess Kinyah,

At the age of three, I understood who I was supposed to be in your life, but what I didn't know was who you would become to the world. Like me, all parents believe their children are special and unique; however, I knew you were special. Your intellectual abilities for your age were far beyond your peers and various tests and challenges continue to prove how intellectually gifted you are. Along with the challenges that come with being gifted, you suffered with your health. By the age of five, you had already had six surgeries on your nose. The surgeries were designed to stop the consistent bleeding you experienced on a daily basis. However, every time we had to go to the doctor, I never really understood what was going on inside of you, but now I know that you had to endure everything thus far to help create the message and ministry you have today. Your ability to relate to other children on various levels is what helps create and nurture the relationship you have with others.

Kinyah, the journey that you are about to take has everything to do with why you suffered so much. Blood is the gift of life. The oxygen that is found in blood helps your body get nutrients and water and provides life. Without blood, there is no life. The blood you shed at a young age was symbolic to the life you were releasing into others. Now, years later, you have been graced with the Blood of Jesus to help **resuscitate** the lives of others through your message and journey. The pain you endured during surgery was to build your strength for the journey that you are embarking upon now. The pain that you felt was given to you as a memory so that you will connect with those you will reach. As you already know, B Chill Lemonade is just your podium and not your message. I am so proud of you for running this race. It will not be easy, but it will be fulfilling. A lot of people often ask, "Where are the true leaders?" I am glad to say that I have been privileged to father one and her name is Kinyah Bean. As an individual, you might never fit in, so don't try. I encourage you to be brave and stand out.

Love,

Your Daddy

Demetrius Braddock

TABLE OF CONTENTS

CHAPTER ONE

MY STORY

Hello, my name is Kinyah Bean and I have several nicknames, but the one I love the most is KB. I am the 8-year-old owner and CEO of B Chill Lemonade, LLC and future dentist. I am a lover of cheetahs because of their speed and abilities and traveling is a huge passion of mine. I have been to Bridgeport, Atlanta, Huntsville, New York, Jackson, Durant and have plans to become an international traveler as well. I was born in Memphis, Tennessee at Baptist Women's Hospital and delivered by Dr. Monica Pasley, an OB/GYN. She took care of my mom and me before I was born.

Upon my arrival, I was greeted by Dr. Bianca Sweeten, my amazing pediatrician. She has been a consistent medical influence in my life, no matter what city or state I have lived in with my family. While living in Memphis, I was a member of St. Andrew AME Church under

Pastors Dr. Kenneth and Marilyn Robinson and New Friendship MBC Church under Pastors Paul and Debra Reed. My mom and I were very active in New Friendship. My mom was the choir vice-president and leader of the dance ministry. When I was about two, I enjoyed the King's Kids Choir that was for children under 12. I do not have a lot of memories of Memphis, but I know I had a great start.

Life in Memphis did not last long because at around the age of three we relocated to Nashville, Tennessee after the birth of my baby brother, Demetrius Braddock II. Growing up in Nashville was awesome! I was involved in various activities such as Girl Scouts, ballet and gymnastics at the Nashville School of Dance and Music, track and field on the Illusions track team and I also played soccer. Plus, I made two of the world's greatest friends, Quincee Etheridge and Laila Hentrel. My time with my best friends was always full of laughter, joy, tears, problems and solutions. We loved each other and did everything together everyday, including various community activities.

While being involved in the community, I excelled academically as a student at Eakin Elementary School where I started at the age of 4 years old. I owe my academic foundation to my exceptional elementary school teachers, Mrs. Frye, Mrs. See and Mrs. Bunt. During my time in Nashville, I learned much about myself. I discovered that my favorite color was purple. Purple means royalty and my father always called me his "Princess," so I knew that I was someone who mattered and had value. It's also special to me because it's my Grandmother Marcia's favorite color, too. My friendships with Quincee and Laila exposed me to various literature and chapter books since we read a lot. Some of my favorite series of books to read are from the Magic Tree House Books. These books are awesome. They provide mysteries, adventure and fun for all readers. My friends and I started a book club where we would meet, eat and read books. I was always sad when our busy schedules forced us to cancel club meetings, but it never stopped us from reading during after school care at Eakin Harris Hillman.

While hanging out with my friends was one of my main pleasures, I also enjoyed dancing, singing, swimming, spending time with my family and doing anything that brought me laughter and joy. Even though I do not get to watch much television, some of my favorite shows are *Descendants* and *The Flash*. I thoroughly enjoy the music and plot of *Descendants* and what makes *The Flash* so special is I watch it with my dad. Watching television shows in my house is not just about sitting and watching quietly. We discuss every detail of the show and even predict what we believe will happen in future scenes. This is truly one of my favorite things to do when I am free.

Loving my family, living life and enjoying my friends all brought great joy to me daily until we moved to Flowood, Mississippi where I had to start over again at a new school, Flowood Elementary, make new friends and live in a new community. My family and I moved to support my mom as a student at Mississippi College School of Law. This transition was very quick, but hard. I was away on summer break visiting my family in Memphis when my mom found out she was accepted in to law school and needed to relocate very soon. Because of this, I was not able to say good-bye to my best friends and their families. This was devastating to me and was a very difficult adjustment.

I attended a new school, Flowood Elementary, and hoped I would make a lot of friends to help with the transition, but that didn't happen. Although I did not make a lot of new friends, my teacher, Mrs. Lambert was exceptional and I truly enjoyed her class. She made learning fun by putting our skills and concepts into songs and raps. Not having a lot of friends, I found myself enjoying my little brother more than I had before. Demetrius and I would ride our bikes for hours outside; we played in the dirt, built castles with blocks, drew and colored pictures, read books together and learned to provide great support for each other, especially when we were in trouble. Living in Flowood gave me more time to dream and think about my future since I saw my mom pursuing her dreams. I truly learned how to dream while living in Flowood and I fell in love with makeup and accessories. I acted in the house, played dress up and pretended that I was walking on the red carpet.

While learning to dream and my mom being a law student, I was also exposed to the challenges various communities and cultures face with the justice system, lack of resources, childhood hunger and violence. As a believer and a Christian, I have always been concerned about the level of violence around the world. During car rides to and from school or other places with my family, I can remember questioning the behavior of others from television shows that my parents watched such as local news, First 48, NCIS and other crime dramas.

These shows depict various bad behaviors from those in the community such as murder, robbery, gun violence, fighting, etc. I found myself praying for the community and world that God would help us make better choices. In times such as those, I remember my parents covering my brother and me in prayer and asking that God would protect our family and our friends from hurt, harm and danger, which He did. Since those concerns still affect me today, I continue to pray for others and ask God to do the same for them. I demonstrate love and respect for others simply because I believe they are both a part of the answers to our problems. They might not solve everything, but I know they will help reduce the amount of crime in the world. I pray that I can be a contributing factor to helping reduce violence, especially among youth.

Due to the level of concern I have for our world, I desire to use my business and my message to inspire the community, bring hope to families and influence the blueprint of my generation.

I am Kinyah Bean, CEO of B Chill Lemonade, LLC.

CHAPTER TWO

HOW IT ALL BEGAN

In the fall of 2015, at the age of 6, while living in Nashville, my father challenged me to start my own company by the age of 10. Unsure of how to start a business, or the true meaning of a business, I went to my mom and asked her questions. I wanted something a little kid could do because, after all, I was only in the 1st grade at Eakin Elementary School. Running a business by the age of 10 was not something my friends and I thought could happen. My mom and I talked about a lot of ideas that could turn into a business, such as selling art since I love drawing or selling homemade ice cream since that was a treat my family enjoyed every Sunday. I chose to explore an ice cream business. Originally, I was fascinated with the idea of doing my own ice cream shop where I would sell different flavors. But, I was unsure if it was something I could do since I was so young. So, my mom and I researched how to start an ice cream company.

I explored this option by speaking with owners of local ice cream shops, such as franchise owners from Baskin-Robbins, to get an idea of how to start and what I needed. During my time of research with my mom and the business owners, I was able to ask all kinds of questions about what I needed to do to become a Baskin-Robbins franchisee. They suggested that my family and I look into various ice cream shop models to see which one would be best from a financial point of view, while looking at the flavors I would love to sell. After multiple discussions, my Grandmother Marcia and I began thinking of flavors we could make for my ice cream company. We decided that we would put the ice cream on a marble slab, which is frozen and is used to help mix the flavors with various toppings, all while remaining frozen and cold.

We came up with the name B Kool Creamery by using the initial from my last name, Bean, which is B and a word that described how the ice cream made you feel, Kool. And creamery was how I wanted the texture of the ice cream to be. We were thinking of doing different versions of chocolate and pistachio and we considered asking family members to share their favorite flavors, so we could have a variety. But, it took too much time to try each flavor because I was very busy in school, so we put the idea of an ice cream business on hold. After that, I got involved in more activities at my school and in the community, like Girl Scouts, track and field, gymnastics and soccer. As time went by I still thought about the idea of owning my own ice cream shop, but I did not work on making that company a reality.

In August of 2016, my family and I moved to Flowood, Mississippi to support my mom while she was pursuing her dreams in law school. I was not really focusing on much outside of my schoolwork and I enjoyed family time the most. Moving to Flowood was very difficult for me. I was attending a new school, living in a new neighborhood and trying to make new friends, all of which I was not ready to do. My friends from Nashville and I basically grew up together. None of us had family in Nashville, so we all became close like family and moving away from that was not easy.

When God Spoke to Me

On January 16, 2017 while living in Flowood, I was bored watching television while enjoying the day off from school in observance of the Martin Luther King Jr. Holiday. I was thirsty and wanted something different to drink, so I went in the kitchen and made a glass of fresh lemonade for myself. God gave me an idea. I heard his voice five times and the images in my head were in 3D on how the lemonade should be made. God said, "Get sugar, water and lemons." The images and voices were so strong that I could see myself making the lemonade before even going into the kitchen. He gave me the instructions in a vision and I got up, went in the kitchen without permission and made the lemonade. Usually, I did not need to ask to go in the kitchen; for my own safety, my parents always told me to ask them to cut things that required a knife, unless I could use scissors.

After making the lemonade, I placed it on the counter and I went to clean my room, as instructed by my mom. I went back for my lemonade and it was gone. I asked what happened and my mom said, "Your dad drank your lemonade." My dad, not knowing that I had made the lemonade, said that he would take me back to Chick-fil-A to get more. I told him that I didn't go to Chick-fil-A and I had made the lemonade myself! Shocked at how good it tasted, my father and mother asked if I remembered how to make the lemonade and I said I did. In trying to answer my parents, I was amazed at how much my dad liked the lemonade because I was only trying to make myself something different to drink and I wasn't thinking it would be that good.

The Start of B Chill Lemonade, LLC

My mom, dad and brother were in the kitchen with me. We were all laughing about the lemonade and my mom asked if this was the business idea that I would like to pursue. I said of course I would love to make lemonade. My mom and I went to the dinner table; she got her laptop and typed up 60 flyers advertising my company. She asked me what flavors I would like to start with and I responded with original, mango, coconut, raspberry, strawberry with all of them in diet as well.

We went outside and my mom, brother and I prayed in a circle, holding hands over the flyers. I prayed over each flyer as I excitedly placed them on 60 cars in my neighborhood.

Kool Lemonade
by Kinyah

My name is Kinyah and I am exploring the world of entrepreneurship. To start learning mor
about starting and running a business, I have decided to sell lemonade. My business will off
fresh squeezed lemonade along with various flavors. The flavors that I will provide are cocor
lemonade, strawberry lemonade, original lemonade, diet lemonade (with Splenda) and raspbe
lemonade. Other flavors and garnishes are available upon request. I am willing to sell the
lemonade by the glass (cup) or in a gallon jug. Please text or call for prices and orders.
(Please allow 24 hours for all lemonade orders)

Thank you for supporting me!! Your business is greatly appreciated.
(901) 871-8782

It was past dinnertime, but my family patiently waited for me. We then went out to eat, but all I could think about was if I had any orders of lemonade. I literally asked my mom over and over if anyone had placed an order yet and finally that night someone did! I had my first order for five gallons from my mom's law school classmate, Brittany Brown. Her message was received on Monday, January 16, 2017 at 6:57 pm and it said:

> "I would like to order five gallons!!! One diet lemonade, one strawberry lemonade, two regular lemonades, and one of whatever her favorite is!"

I was so thrilled because this was the first $30.00 that my company made! I was so excited and anxious that I could barely eat dinner because I was thinking about my first order. I did not know that my mom had shared my new business venture with many of the contacts in her phone, which I later found out is how Ms. Brown knew about my company. After discussing how this lemonade could be a staple in our community, we researched how we could fulfill the orders with high quality products. We went to Kroger in Pearl, Mississippi and shopped for different flavors. I decided that I would use syrups to help flavor the lemonade. We purchased a lot of lemons and other ingredients from Kroger that were very expensive, but we knew it would pay off. We used the ingredients and worked on the recipe over and over again. Since I had only made one glass of lemonade for myself, I had to learn how to convert the amount and measurements I used for 8 ounces into 128 ounces.

The amount of math skills that we had to use taught us all new things about fractions, conversions and measurements. My father actually shared that he learned more about those math skills making lemonade than he ever did sitting in a class. Once we created a recipe that we believed worked, we started to see an increase in orders. After using the flavors and getting the reviews from customers, my mom explained to me that for every pre-made flavor we used we would need to pay other companies for their products. I decided immediately that I did not want to pay anyone for the ingredients, except for necessary items like fruit. So, I told my mom we would not use the syrups anymore because I wanted to use fresh fruit.

To help finalize the recipe, my family and I did a Pop-Up Shop at New Jerusalem Baptist Church in Memphis on January 28, 2017. The feedback from family, friends, chefs, restaurant owners and business professionals was priceless. They rated my lemonade on sweetness, tartness, texture, flavor and overall appearance. We used the feedback and after much work, changes and test samples, we finally got our unique flavor of lemonade, which is now referred to as "liquid gold," amazing fresh squeezed lemonade everyone has grown to love and support. The name "liquid gold" came from customer comments about the color of the lemonade, as having a "goldish" look and the flavor was as good as gold!

How I Got the Name B Chill Lemonade

Because of the positive response from the community, we had to make some business decisions to secure my idea by starting with the company's name. The original company name was B Kool Lemonade, but since that was the name of my ice cream shop idea my dad suggested we change the name to B Chill Lemonade. This would allow me to use the B Kool name if I ever open an ice cream shop. My mom helped me get my business licenses and we saw how her law school training could benefit us. On Thursday, January 26, 2017 my company, B Chill Lemonade, was registered as an LLC (Limited Liability Company) and we received our FEIN (Federal Employer Identification Number). Filing those documents was exciting for us as a family and me as a business owner. On a mission to secure my company, my family and I created the Business Plan and Operating Agreement on February 6, 2017. These additional documents allowed B Chill Lemonade to start functioning on a higher level, rather than just being considered as a lemonade stand.

Using the reputation of my products and my business credentials, I was able to start selling lemonade by the cup at The Mississippi Farmer's Market in Jackson, the state capital. This was the first stationary location that my lemonade could be found. I was thrilled, nervous and scared, all at the same time! I did not know how other people would respond to the lemonade, how hard I would have to work to get people to come and try my lemonade and the effort that it would take to prepare, set up and break down the booth for this weekly event. This was all very important because it is how B Chill Lemonade started as a real business.

CHAPTER THREE

LIFE AS A KID CEO

It has been an awesome experience being an 8-year-old business owner. I have enjoyed the privilege of traveling, exploring cultures and communities and experiencing a lot of other things such as music and food. As a business owner, I had to adjust to the challenges of sacrificing time with my family and friends, while reducing the amount of sleep so I can make sure I complete orders for lemonade, do school assignments and participate in hobbies and events. I wouldn't trade this opportunity for anything in the world because of all the growth I have experienced in my life. This has helped me develop the tenacity needed to not quit and be successful. I have learned not to give up and to stay motivated, even when it gets difficult and things are not going my way. My life will never be the same because of all I have learned while on this journey.

When becoming a business owner, one of my first challenges was trying to figure out how much money it would take to start the company. These funds are called "start-up costs." Before starting B Chill Lemonade, we had to consider the cost of a business license, ingredients, advertising, marketing, logo and other necessities. After creating a business plan that outlined the company, my family knew that I was very serious about being a business owner and they invested the first $500.00 to start B Chill Lemonade. Although those funds only covered the basics, it allowed me to get going and the company began to have a lot of orders and was able to take care of the financial needs as we grew.

A Family-Operated Business

In thinking about the start-up costs, one thing you must consider is staff. Hiring people is necessary for the efficiency of your company. Thankfully, my family had various career and educational experiences that I could use to assist me with the initial needs of the company.

My father, Demetrius, is the CFO (Chief Financial Officer) of B Chill Lemonade. He handles all of the financial obligations, such as paying bills and balancing the bank account. My mother, Valerie, is the COO (Chief Operating Officer). She is responsible for the day-to-day operations of B Chill Lemonade. Her duties include, but are not limited to: handling all details for events; daily lemonade inventory and orders; shopping for materials, ingredients and supplies; assisting me in keeping up with social media outlets; maintaining cleaning supplies; stocking all supplies; and helping me respond to event requests and manage my calendar. My brother, Demetrius, is the Manager. He has been taught various tasks that he is able to perform that are age-appropriate. He is usually required to count the inventory, pack the bags and make sure we have everything that is on the list. Without all of them helping, there would be no B Chill Lemonade!

Even with the help of my family, I usually average 20-40 hours a week dedicated to the business. This can vary because some weeks are busier than others. My mom keeps an outline of events that we need to prepare for and a list of orders that need to be filled. This helps us be more efficient and not waste time. The major activities are: pressing lemons, which takes the most time when preparing lemonade; cleaning supplies and materials; and setting up for events and breaking down afterwards. The weekly hours can also increase when I have to travel and prepare for presentations and speaking engagements. The time of the year can also influence how many hours I might work during a week. This is because I usually have more to do in summer months. We go to family reunions and other parties and since it is hot, lemonade is a cool, refreshing beverage of choice, so there is more demand. Even with the seasons changing, I have been blessed to have consistent business for my lemonade and I am always working to make sure the company has year-round sales.

Because of the success of B Chill Lemonade, I am also invited to various events for vending opportunities. When you are a vendor, you compete with other small business owners who are also using the event to showcase their product or service. Opportunities like this happen all over the country. I am grateful that I have been able to travel and meet so many people. Usually when traveling, I enjoy cuisine from the local communities, network with other business owners, meet people from the local government such as the mayor and state officials, enjoy the events and festivals and sight see with my family. I am grateful for each chance I get to explore new places. I look forward to traveling internationally as I strive to expand the company to a global level.

Branding

Marketing and branding are very important when starting your own business. What we have learned is that not all strategies for marketing and branding work for every company and you have to figure out which strategies work for you. In order for B Chill Lemonade to be recognized as a legitimate company, I knew we needed a symbol or logo that would identify our company. My first logo was drawn by two local teens in Jackson, Mississippi where I selected the one that best represented my idea for the company. My father and I gave the teens suggestions and ideas and the one that captured the concept the best was the winner. The winning artist was Vleary Washington. Her design replicated my ideas as a whole.

After selecting the logo, we were able to begin purchasing materials and items that we could put the logo on and use to help market the company, like shirts, bags, mugs and a banner.

Shortly after the company began to expand, my family and I decided that we needed a more mainstream logo that reflected my personality and my overall desire to provide a high quality product. I wanted a symbol that could catch the eye of the customer, have a great slogan and represent me. The logo I chose was awesome and I loved everything about it.

The business was growing quickly, so we had a professional do a company analysis to make sure we were still on the right track, since things were starting to move fast. The report suggested that we reconsider the logo since it could pose a problem in the future with another lemonade company. Although the two companies were not the same and the bees were not identical, nor closely related in presentation, we wanted to eliminate any possibility of infringement or legal concerns. This was a tough decision to make since I truly loved the previous logo. After much thought, we changed the logo to a lemon drinking lemonade. This logo is very fun and has many opportunities to help my company remain distinct and trendy. The lemon drinking lemonade also helped us develop the slogan: "B Chill Lemonade…so good, even lemons drink it!" The lemon displays my sassiness, personality, hair and love for accessories and being a girl. I really liked this new logo, but I still wanted the previous logo of a bee drinking the lemonade. After much discussion and consulting a trademark attorney, we finally decided that having the bee drinking lemonade was not going to pose a threat and would be our final logo for B Chill Lemonade. Since we kept the lemon logo, we have decided upon another business venture to use that logo. This process of choosing the best logo to represent us was time consuming and not cost efficient; however, it was necessary to make sure the brand had an identity and presence.

When thinking about your logo, you want something that represents your company as a whole and not just a certain part. The logo should be distinct from other companies and unique to the services or products that reflect your business. Once you choose the logo, branding the company is easy. I use the logo on everything: email, website, social media, shirts, bags, etc. Everything must be uniform and scream B Chill Lemonade. I am always looking for ways to increase marketing and branding and usually those ways are discovered when I travel and vend.

The journey and process that I have shared with you has definitely not been an easy one. The most challenging areas are balancing between being an owner of a company and a student in school. Both tasks are very demanding and require a lot of my time, but I am able to be successful because of my support system. Usually one or two days during the week, my grandmother, Marcia, will come and assist my family in housecleaning and she will help my brother and me with homework. This frees up my mom to finish her various responsibilities in and out of the business.

I also attend tutoring by Dr. Eddie "Coach" Yancy on Thursdays. He is absolutely amazing. Because of my tutoring, I can travel and cover concepts I might have missed in school during my time away. My parents are also certified teachers, so they help my brother and me with our schoolwork. My mom usually outlines my schedule for school and the business so we can stay focused. During the week we also try not to deviate from our plans, so we can stay on track and be balanced with what we have to do. This seems very rigid, but it is necessary to be successful with school and the company. The most important key to balancing them both is organization.

I do my best to maintain efficiency and excellence in my company, along with success in the classroom since my parents said if my grades go down, they would close the company until I am back at the level of their high expectations. I do not want to ever close the business because of poor performance in school!

I want to establish B Chill Lemonade on all seven continents, which means that I must stay organized and balanced to succeed. Even though this company has not been open long, it has been profitable in more ways than one. It has taught me the importance of balance, drive and perseverance, all of which should be life-long traits. I choose to be a hardworking business owner. I plan to continue on the path of being an entrepreneur because of the freedom it provides me as I learn and grow. I am able to write my own destiny freely without the restrictions of another person's ideas and expectations of me. I am a free functioning entrepreneur and I love it!

CHAPTER FOUR

MY INSPIRATIONS

My inspirations are God, my family and my friends. I rely on them all to help me push through the hard times and be there to celebrate every level of success. I use them as wise counsel when it is time to make decisions, especially when it involves my personal life and the company. They are my rock and all of them are dependable and reliable.

God

God is so inspirational to me. He shows me new ways to love and grow every day. To get a better understanding of God and how He loves other people, I read his word that tells me how Jesus died for our sins, which makes me feel important and loved. Reading the scriptures is like a manual on how to live and treat other people. If we follow the manual we will have better lives.

I feel safe and nothing is more important than my time with God. When I am home, I usually spend time with God in my bedroom and in my living room. If not, I can spend a lot of time with him at church. I can't remember a specific or great experience with God because they are all awesome. I feel so special because God communicates with me.

During my time with Christ, He shows me various images concerning my life. He talks with me and our time together is priceless. Another amazing thing that I love about God is how He is concerned about me. Once I was sick and not feeling well and when I asked him to heal me by his stripes, He did. I didn't feel better right away, but I did feel better the more I prayed and trusted that He would heal me. God is amazing. When I spend time with Jesus, I enjoy writing songs and poetry that reflect how I feel about him. Here's a song I wrote during the summer of 2017:

Love for Christ

I think about him all the time. I can't get him out of my mind. He's there when I need him the most; He left me a comforter, the Holy Ghost. He saved my life. Christ should win a Nobel Peace Prize. I have been saved from sin. Skies shine so so bright. Oh, Oh, Oh, He's my friend, Jesus Christ.

Jesus is my everything. The same love that I have for God is the same love I have for YOU!

A Dad Like You

My dad inspires me because he followed his dreams of becoming a teacher and eventually will open his own school. I am fortunate to have a dad like him. Our relationship is so amazing. He is always there when I need him. When I feel down he knows just what to say to lift me up. When I feel weak it is in him I feel strong. He encourages me to be the best I can be. He is a great example for me and shows me so much love, respect and support. I am so grateful God thought enough of me to send Daddy my way to help me reach my full potential. Because of his challenge to me to own my own company before I was 10 years old, I am able to continue on every day.

The greatest experiences with my dad are during our Daddy/Daughter date nights. I usually get all dressed up and wait for my father to come in a suit or tuxedo and it's just my dad and me. He has flowers for me and we eat at a nice restaurant. We talk, laugh, cry and enjoy our time together. We usually end with a horse ride downtown and enjoy a sweet dessert before we go home. It is so wonderful because we are alone during this time. My mom respects this time by not calling us at all once she has helped me get dolled up and opens the door for my father to receive my hand. I love these moments with my dad because they assure me I am valuable and I matter.

My Selfless Mother

My mom inspires me every day. She embraces all of her dreams and does not allow obstacles or trials to stop her from being her best. Watching my mom juggle all that she does for my company, our family and herself shows me how important our roles are as the women in the house. The love and selflessness that my mom has for me allows me to dream freely and become who I was created to be. She pushes me daily to not take no for an answer and to create my own way when a door has been closed. My mom has sacrificed so much for me to pursue my dreams as a business owner that she gave up her dream to become a lawyer. I am unsure if I could ever re-pay her, but I am certain that if I stay on this path, I will continue to make her smile. Her example encourages me to be a creative thinker and problem solver. My mom is a prayer warrior. She prays for us as a family daily and shares what God says about us.

Every day is amazing with my mom. We paint nails, laugh, joke, cook and wash clothes. She teaches me everything I need to know so I can be self-sufficient. My scariest moments are to see my mom upset, even though I learn positive ways to respond to situations from watching her. I love and appreciate my mom so much!

I Love You the Way You Are

I absolutely love my brother, Demetrius Braddock II. He inspires me to dream freely because he has so many dreams himself, but is not concerned about what others think or say. Demetrius wants to have his own lawn care service, build mansions and castles, design airplanes and do many great things. He is teaching me how to be free. A lot of times, I am concerned about what a person might think about me, but he always says, "Sissy.... do not worry about them. I am your friend and I love you just the way you are." This means so much to me. He has a way of loving me when I feel misunderstood. We pray together, laugh together and sometimes get in trouble together! My brother's self-confidence at 5 years old helps me to think very highly of myself. He believes he's the best in everything he does, which motivates me when I find flaws in myself. My greatest moment with D was when I held him for the first time on April 20, 2012. I fed him a bottle and my life changed forever.

As you can see, I rely on my family for inspiration every day to help me achieve, overcome, persevere and be the best person I can be. It's not always easy, but I highly recommend that you find cheerleaders on your road to success.

Ya Ya

My grandmother, Marcia Smith ("Ya Ya"), has always been there for me in so many ways. She always makes herself available to help me with homework, my emotions, my successes and anything I might experience in life. She inspires me with her unconditional love. The amount of support Ya Ya gives me is priceless. She is there to motivate me and to push me when it gets tough. She provides strategies to help with rejection and what I might think are failures. Her prayers and songs are always there to help bring joy to my day and assist me in seeing the bright side in every situation. Her optimistic personality helps me believe that I can achieve anything I put my mind to. No matter how much I might fall, she is always there to catch me and love me through it all. I love my Ya Ya.

Paw Paw

My grandfather, Carson Smith ("Paw Paw"), is a man of few words. He demonstrates his support by always encouraging me to be my best. He shows me how much he loves me by taking care of my grandmother and allowing her to spend lots of time with me at events or to help make lemonade. Paw Paw is very understanding and knows how important it is for us to have Ya Ya's help. He works a lot, but is always there to show my family and me a great time. He is a true example of a hard worker that I cherish dearly. I love my Paw Paw.

Gi Gi

My dad's mom, Angela Braddock ("Gi Gi"), is very special to me. I am inspired by how hard she works to take care of her family and my family as well. She opened her home to us to make, store and sell lemonade to our customers. Gi Gi is always willing to lend a helping hand anyway that she can. I appreciate the love and support she gives us as we are developing B Chill Lemonade. I love my Gi Gi.

Gi Paw

My dad's father, Larry Braddock ("Gi Paw"), has everything. All the equipment we have ever needed is at his house. He provides us with generators, nails, boards and bricks. His ability to have what we need is what inspires me. I want to be in a position to be used by God by having what people need to pursue their dreams. I appreciate the love and support he gives to my family and me. I love my Gi Paw.

All of my grandparents give freely of their time and resources to help me build B Chill Lemonade. Their support comes in different shapes, forms and fashions. They all give so much of themselves and I appreciate them.

It Takes a Village

I have been privileged to live in different communities since I was born. I have lived in Memphis, Tennessee; Nashville, Tennessee; and Flowood, Mississippi. Every place had neighborhoods made up of amazing people, great food and a love for a great time. There were times I witnessed adversity where families suffered loss and tragedy. I've learned many lessons from the hardships I saw in those communities. I've also learned I can overcome anything I face, as long as I have the right people in my life helping me. Now I am chillin' my way to success!

CHAPTER FIVE

CHANGING THE WORLD

I want to inspire my generation to become bold entrepreneurs who are prepared to lead our country. I will use my voice to inspire and transform the minds of my peers. I desire to use my gifts as an example of love. I will use my business as a platform to raise awareness and seek solutions surrounding youth issues. I will get involved with youth organizations to help provide solutions to problems such as childhood hunger and violence. I desire to create a space where we feel our voices are heard and will contribute to the positive outcomes of our communities.

Being an entrepreneur provides open doors and access to people that will accept my voice and message for inspiration, motivation and guidance. B Chill Lemonade plans to expand so we can positively impact families and communities by increasing financial stability through employment. B Chill Lemonade will be a model that provides employees high standards in communication, customer service and opportunities for professional growth and development.

Globally, my company will be able to support communities in need by sharing our resources to help them grow and become self-sufficient. I would love to provide educational facilities that will help those in need and inspire them to change their lives and become successful.

Business Museum

I hope to change the lives of kids by increasing opportunities for them to grow and learn. My mission is to create a community network system that closes the gap between young dreamers and current entrepreneurs. My efforts to help kids will be based on offering internships and being a source of help that can build relationships with people that have interests in a variety of fields. I want kids to know that even though they are young, they still have a voice.

Once, while traveling through Memphis, I created a concept for a Business Museum. It could include classrooms and office space for various occupations such as doctors, dentists and massage therapists. The offices would be operated by volunteer professionals who are willing to assist youth in learning more about their fields of interest. The museum could also have a movie theater that plays documentaries about how companies began and how they made changes as they grew. There would also be other entertainment features, like food courts (operated by the young people) and sports activities. The museum would be a place where kids could have fun and learn at the same time. I would call the museum "Pieces of the Future" because it would offer pieces of opportunities that could help shape the future of young people.

CHAPTER SIX

YOU CAN DO IT, TOO!

A "kidpreneur" is a kid that follows their dreams or uses their gifts and talents to start their own business. An entrepreneur participates in all of the day-to-day activities it takes to run a company. I was invited to the Sweet Auburn Music Festival in Atlanta, Georgia and had to prepare lemonade for 1,000 people! In preparation for this major event, my family and I had a meeting to discuss what was necessary to make all of the lemonade we would need. We averaged how many servings we could get out of one gallon and determined how many boxes of lemons we needed. We recruited family and friends to help us press all of the lemons.

My family support is necessary because of the labor intensive work required by the commercial press we use. My family's participation allows each of us to take turns pressing without getting tired.

To finalize all of the plans before we left, I checked the inventory of lemonade, flavors, supplies and materials to ensure that we had enough for our projected number of customers. I usually go through a checklist to make sure that I do not forget to include items we might need for set up, display, serving or clean up. This is the most important job in this process because it could impact the efficiency of our service and the quality of the lemonade. We also had to create a timeline so that we could be sure we left Memphis in enough time to get to Atlanta. The trip was a 2-day journey and I was responsible for assisting my mom with lodging plans. Once we arrived in Atlanta, I helped transport everything for our set-up. We had to unload the truck and set up the tent, tables, lemonade, flavors, decorations, business cards, trashcan, etc. I also checked the inventory to make sure nothing was damaged during travel. After everything was done, we were ready for customers.

At the end of every event there is a breakdown process. If we are staying for multiple days, certain things are broken down, washed and brought back for the next day, while other supplies remain safely locked under the tent.

Either way, the breakdown process usually has the same level of difficulty and precision required as the packing and set up process.

As you can see, even a kid entrepreneur has a lot of responsibilities!

As a young dreamer you can use your favorite hobbies, talents or gifts to help explore entrepreneurship. My gifts and hobbies are singing, dancing, helping people, drawing and public speaking. These gifts and talents allow me to interact with others, express my love for music through dance, relieve stress and help my community. As youths, we are created with gifts and talents that we can use to develop opportunities, increase revenue and promote change.

Discovering My Business

Many young people ask me all the time:

1. *How do I find out what I can do?* Make a list of all your hobbies or fun things you like to do. For example, I enjoy getting to know new people.

2. *How do I know what my gifts are?* Make a list of all the things you are good at. For example, I am good at speaking.

3. *Can we have a purpose at such a young age?* Yes! Our first purpose is to be kids, students and dreamers. As youth, we can use our imaginations to create whatever we want. When we follow our dreams as youth we are able to be free and express ourselves. My dreams are to be a singer, become a dentist and own my own dental practice.

No matter what your age is, I encourage you to ask God through prayer to show you your purpose, gifts and talents. You can also search within yourself to identify any gifts or talents you can use to start your own business.

Searching Within Yourself

When searching within yourself you should look for hobbies you enjoy doing the most. Think about activities you do every day that you are really good at. If you are good with animals, you might want to pet sit for your neighbors while they are at work or away on vacation.

Once you create a list of these hobbies and talents you will discover that your next step is to choose which gift or talent you could turn into a business. The best choices are the ones that solve a problem in your community. So, think of a need that your community has that your hobbies and talents can answer. It could simply come from a list of hobbies you enjoy or food you can make and love to eat. Once you make a choice you are then on your way to a business idea.

Here is a list of ideas you can easily turn into a business:
- Sell homemade hot chocolate
- Make soap
- Make lotions
- Sell slime
- Sell cookies, brownies and other treats
- Sell art
- Babysit
- Walk dogs
- Cut grass
- Wash cars
- Make snow cones
- Tutor

Challenges to Starting a Business

Although all of these ideas are fun and easy, there are always challenges when starting your own business. Some of the challenges that I face the most are: fear of failure; being rejected by customers; and making new friends who will accept me and understand me as I am. These challenges affect my emotions and my momentum. I never knew how much influence people had over how I felt until I started B Chill Lemonade.

To handle these challenges, I am learning to love myself and be secure in my dreams, abilities and company. I surround myself with positive people who support me when I am down. I stay focused on my dreams, no matter how hard the journey might be at times. I use singing and dancing as a way to help relieve frustration and handle my challenges. I also use my fears as motivation to overcome and persevere. If we allow our fears, obstacles and negative experiences to rule us we will never be who God created us to be. We are special and so are our dreams and goals. When I am down and feel myself struggling with this journey I read my favorite scripture, Psalm 23:1-2:

1. *The Lord is my Shepherd;*
   I shall not want.

2. *He makes me lie down in green pastures;*
   He leads me beside the still waters.

Here is my interpretation:

- *Lord* = Savior from sin.
- *Shepherd* = He takes care of me and leads me.
- *I shall not want* = God gives me what I need and I don't need anything else. He is going to protect me and provide for me.

The Psalms are like a contract between you and God. It is God saying what he will do for you and he will never break his promises. I encourage you today to know that your gifts, hobbies and dreams matter.

You are never too young to start your own business! If I can do it, you can do it, too!!!

Dear Reader,

Have you noticed all of the negative issues impacting kids in our communities?

- Bullying
- Hatred
- Homelessness
- Suicide
- Adoptions and foster care
- Hunger

Can you guess what the solution is for these problems? **LOVE!**

Love, is defined as "a strong affection for another arising out of kinship or personalities." The Bible says, "Love is patient, love is kind." It does not envy, it does not boast, it is not proud. It does not dishonor others, it is not self-seeking, it is not easily angered; it keeps no record of wrongs. Love does not delight in evil but rejoices with the truth. It always protects, always trusts, always hopes and always perseveres.

I want to encourage you to love one another. If we all begin to exercise love then we would remember to treat others the way we desire to be treated. Don't forget, as you take steps to make a difference in the world, you can't do it without LOVE. Start your difference with LOVE today.

Love Always,

Kinyah Bean

B Chill Lemonade, LLC

B Chill Lemonade is a licensed beverage company that provides authentic, hand-squeezed lemonade with fresh fruit for tantalizing flavors. This beverage is prepared and served for occasions and events of all sizes. The flavors are blueberry, coconut, mango, peach, raspberry, strawberry and original. Each flavor is prepared with high quality ingredients with every consumer in mind. The fresh fruit flavors are offered in diet, vegan and regular. Each batch is sampled to ensure consistency and high quality control.

What makes this lemonade unique is it is "made with love and family."

To order B Chill Lemonade or invite us to serve at your next event, please call

901-871-8782 or email info@bchilllemonade.com

You may also visit my website for more information: www.bchilllemonade.com

For interviews, speeches, book signings and appearances, please contact:

www.lavaldreams.com

Email: wesleybelle@hotmail.com

Phone 323-957-4820